Alleluia Chorus

Also by Lois Moyles

I Prophesy Survivors

LOIS MOYLES

Alleluia Chorus

new and selected poems

Woolmer/Brotherson Ltd
ANDES, NEW YORK

Published by
WOOLMER/BROTHERSON, LTD., ANDES, NEW YORK 13731
All Rights Reserved
First Printing

Grateful acknowledgment is made to the following publications where
some of these poems first appeared:

The New Yorker: "Thomas in the Fields"
"Report from California"
"A Tale Told by a Head"
"He Knows What He's Doing"

Partisan Review: "Named Lazarus"

Shenandoah: "Art-In-Action" (Copyright © 1974 by Washington
and Lee University, reprinted from *Shenandoah:*
The Washington and Lee University Review
with the permission of the Editor.)

Works: "The Old Customs"
"For the Wars"
"Casualty"
"The Gift of the Perfect Beast"
"Once Like Adam"
"My Innocence"

CONTENTS

ALLELUIA CHORUS 1

I
Superb lawns are steady in their oncoming,
no amount of mowing can stop them.
However repetitious,
no starfire or heavy rainbow trained on them
                    can dull their blades.
So far, the sheer quantity of green attended
has exhausted eleven queens.

II
Who's keeping track of the details?
Down bus-aisles that dwindle to smoke,
backwards to birth,
                    astronomers go, and commuters
riding sunlit ovals into town.
To mingle with metals,
to get the feel of real keys
and the tiny muscles that work the words.

III
Pepys is dead,
but the upstream-hours he released
are still monitored for weight
                    and speed of passage.
The sky beating against his table
                    exposed the future even then,
flapping its blueprint noisily,
                    exposed *us*:

IV
Runners down unearned streets
searching for a safehouse in this century.
Or for some featureless fold in the brain
where voluminous notes might be hidden.
At sun-up secret police are awakened
by multitudes bending the shadows flat.
It's hard to keep track of all that,
but advances are made,
and preparers of manuscripts go on,
                                        or around,
like veins repairing themselves.

V

We're careful what issues we raise nowadays.
No more slave ships
            with their terrible tenure of brothers.
No more black babies
            raging at the coldness of water.
Today we demand everything be
            the temperature of tears.
Besides, would we know more if we knew more
about all that blood, salty and
            blind as an eel, that was lost?
And what, different, would we do
about coldwater futures
            rising on the charts, about an inch a year?

VI

We don't embellish ourselves much anymore
who relish an austere god, and very distant..
Humble is more hopeful
leaving room for advancement toward him
                        without impertinence.
Knowing what pain, on our behalf, he would permit
we wear T-shirts made out of beaten-back surroundings,
or old army coats,
to tour the streets where S. Pepys went
                        in his green velvet sleeves.
Streets that turn back on themselves,
            where scarves that have followed for centuries
advance to meet us
            filling our mouths with details.

The road is perfect tonight
and you say to everything in sight,
"Arrive, arrive if you can
and see what it's like to please me."

Old cars overtake you
drawing soft faces after them.
You feel you must follow and defend yourself
for you are proud
and would rather die in a harsh way
than be stolen from.

You will catch them with instruments,
lifting wrists at their thinnest places.
In this wild, impure moonlight
you're like the doctor who dries
        his hands on the backs of sheep,
who makes room for all who grow big as they come
        and are not worn small by the effort,
for the strangers being born
                        unwarranted.

This road that intended nothing
has diminished you.
But you can't seem to stop,
        wired as you are with hired memories.
Like a sun at the end of the day,
you would learn what has to be burned
                to become visible —
and what lost for the light to fall
on the outsides of things . . . .

This evening, old habits fall
    odorless over us all.
What a fat beauty the heart is here
turning like a baritono in its cape!
But how surreal, you say,
    is our modesty —
How false our flat eyes —
You turn away to the future
    where the air still hangs
        like pads before you
    protecting you for a while.
You plot to overthrow the sod.

Mortified by marks where the sun has lain,
your skin grows dark as a negative,
    and deprived wristbands glow.
Oh to be nudists again, you say,
    to be even more unequal!
But gunstocks out of Goya will disabuse you —
Overburdened donkeys will exaggerate your guilt —
Tyrants, you will scream,
but we are all born tyrants —
Only the infantas are not required to change.

We are warning you now:
Put on your clothes with the seams sewn inward;
    their touch does not hurt so much
        as the sight of them fraying.
Keep yourself covered —
Even the tongue (which is, after all,
    an entrail beginning, a private part),
even your eyes
    (located as they are at the mouth of your light),
must sometimes be hidden.
And misinformed nerves will search
the zippered compartments
    filled with freedoms.

For if this is the same Anglo-Saxon moon as before,
the same eye, sickle-shape-seen-from-the-side,

will pry at your surfaces.
Luckily your hubs are all covered like organs;
we would be ashamed to see the primitive lugs
in an age so refined.

This is obscene, you say —
But maybe you're too squeamish.
The old customs have, after all,
fallen like pollen upon us,
imparting to our seed the same nature as their own.
They may not be decent, but
if not with these, then with what
can we mate?

The heiress, lunching in West Marin,
told how she had sequestered gold for her marriage. But
years later, she changed her mind.
Highroads to abortion and mental health
had made her believe in other things
                than her mother had.

Besides, like rain, the stock market was falling,
and, like rain, it rose a little
                at the end of its falling.
But there was no rest from the falling again,
from the resting,
from the burrowing underground.

When in a woolen shawl
                she entered the streets once more,
four masked men waylaid her, but it was
all in fun.
                What could be more fun than gold?

Guerrillas broke through the sun roof that season
                with apparent bombs.
Open-mouthed explosions escaped from the rooms.
Ten years of opening cans was compressed into
                those two moments. And
the Quakers began again their
eyewitnessing of inequities.

"No nation has, so far,
a reputation for decent Tibetan dealings."
But the Generals sank to their knees in Axminsters,
                crying:
"Kill the crops, the cranes will then starve
and the storks will wither away."
The assembly trod lightly on the Mohawks that spring,
while in the halls, runners collapsed
                at the doors and lay silent.
The Queen flexes her august muscles, preparing
for the parade.
                Sidesaddle? Astride? Riding behind?
The requirements are rigorous that lead to dominion!

The embarcaderos are filling with orators;
Downwind the judges frown and the rules are forgotten.
The merchant fleet is gripped by their eyebrows
                and drained of its stores.

Orators are made-over-men, who want something else.
They grow sick of riding the rolling serpent
                of consistency.

"Let us make war after all."
And twelve frozen feet of rope scream out
as the tiny trucks pull away.

The statues are cold this year,
                colder than we can ever remember.
Now, none dares face the dog
                who guards the bridge.
None but the druggist
                with his bagful of arrows.

Protect the orators from the dominions
                that float in the tub like spiders!
Protect the Queen! Whose embroidered body
                even now, advances towards pillows.

Saracen-type sandals are worn here again
but with none of the innocence of their inventors.
A pursestring is pulled, but the hammock
reveals nothing of the absent sleeper.

And an undetermined number of birds
are lighting beside the ferny track
              left by trucks
                filled with soft brown stores
for the wars.

I
So many daylights have been dropped,
 like pure propaganda, on our lines
that even the hawks grow pale,
 their profiles empty as coat hangers.
If the wind can whistle through them,
 unwrinkled, undestined,
then the meat of the matter must not be here—
 and not here the hunger to hunt it.
As a soldier, it is understood
 that I wear my nation like a hood
and execute my acts, anonymous.
But do you understand
 that my thoughts do not clot here
 but run on day and night?
And that my coat grows sticky?

II
Cotton was what the Pharoah was wrapped in:
the flower-fiber of a single summer
 that lasts three thousand years.
The root is dead, the seed, the fruit—
 what a strange difference in durabilities!
How the parts fail separately,
 first the hearts then the souls—
how the feathers wear on and on
 purified of their bird—
and the childbearing animals pursue.
I can't stop these helpless things
headed toward my head, let them come.
Like human transplants, they will find
       no vacancy here.
Only more and more of that condition
 they are already weary of.

III
Here is the shortsleeved nurse of the night
who **rev**eals the heartshaped underarm.
Here an **escap**ed soprano sings, higher
 and **more** beautifully than is necessary.
And, in response to unseen cams,

I grow gentle while others grow fierce.
Blood, balsam of the world, proceed!
    This gauze is eternal!
Perhaps the switch that was used to train my son
has not failed in its courage.
But the *tree* —
The *tree* it would have become is lost.

We have applauded all wolves
        living and dead.
And all bears led away to their lessons.
Especially we have praised
        sheep grazing in cool democracy,
and shepherds
        with wool pulled down over everything.
Even though nothing is imitated
        by that imitation.

Our songs with their
        stratagems of water
have hooked us together in endless amity,
but sometimes there's a pause in the applause
when, like birds behind bars,
        we ponder lost agendas:
Have we done justice to the
        invisible discipline of fish?
To the lying lengthwise
        and never trying to stand?

And what about baserunners waving to crowds?
Or umpires moaning
        like tongueless guns in their fields?
Maybe new sounds are needed —
        or new ecstasies —
to pass through the old ones
        like holders of station.

Our heart's little flaps rejoice
        in wave-motions, not meant,
not gesture certainly, however soothing.
But this river is too fast to be held
        or to be made to wait.
The sheep grow fuzzy with motion.
To understand them, copies must be made
of waters cast in bronze,
and stone lambs grazing on stone lawns,
                to be looked at slowly.

And if this takes too long
we will applaud it all without waiting.
Until tips of blood turn back that are touched,
                              applaud!
So that, like firewood rising
            in a joyous reunion of reds,
we may be warmed for a while
            by the sounds of ourselves
                        cheering.

Now what are they doing?
Women dancing in drum-drenched rooms
       have marked themselves with colors,
but it does not help us to know them.
They say they will not submit anymore
       to the authority of calendars.
They will not shield themselves anymore
       from success
            or from the naked statues of success.

And opposite them dancing are silk-faced men
          overcome by spotlights.
Anglers drawing fish from hollowed waters.
Boatswains in diagonal body-loops
       waving foreign arms.
They continue their becoming
       each adding to the shadow
          at his end.

Disco dancers rarely speak of a Messiah,
or when they do, it is in such a way
         his very whiteness is in doubt.
He is more like a window to them
       that heats and cools
         as their visions pass through him.
And when they praise him it is a warbling of levers
       that open the locks
so a great ship may pass.

They will point out to you the ridges
       left on shoulders of dancers
         where shadows were rubbed off.
They will look for triangles
       which don't exist
and yet draw themselves up
        through the bodies of birds.
They're hoping the next generation can explain —

The babies, maybe,
       come like first-time clouds to our city.

Bred of a lonelier line each year
                    with ungovernable appetites,
They will not be satisfied to be gleaners of pins,
nor threadgatherers,
nor ressurectors of gowns cast off by the altered.
Children of another time-zone
come to collect wild stones for their walls.

Eyelids, half-hiders of truth,
                admit it all incomplete,
chopped into primal parts,
                for a meal made of snapshots.
And still more dancers will be arriving soon
whose place is unknown
                and whose meaning is unmade,
like a blank place in the language
                    that only they can fill.

It's a fertile plot that brought us here,
        flawed, but still
                filled with possibilities.
Who would have ever thought, for instance,
of having new sets of cubs each year
                rolling like tubs in the rows?
Or, having failed in vision, of
fitting the blind with fingers
                like white-woven eyes
to unravel the spot just ahead?
Invention is everything!

Sometimes sounds are heard
                in the foggy-faint dawns,
of things touching that were once
                silent and separate.
It's only the god-machine, we say,
                taking up the plot.
But with such coincidences as
                kisses pressed in pairs on the stairs.
(Think what can be made of those tiny scraps!)

As far back as we can remember
there has been this contraption of
                circling seasons,
which permits shadows to be stacked
                like stones before our faces.
And which encourages sacred beasts to increase,
while still lying without pads, in their places.
(And with what beautiful details of mouth —
                what red and delicate hems
                    hung dangerously open!)
But it's an odd plot indeed
in which the magic formula for daughters
           is the same as for sons in all species,
                regardless of need.

Later on, when hundreds more feel the air
like hair across their faces,
           what will the plot demand?

To keep cool certainly,
    with minds mild-of-movement
            as tropic fans.
We'll put on light clothes
with fingerprints lost in fives among the folds.

We'll become waders, maybe,
            attached at the ankles to others
                in New South Wales.
A good place to replace the emptiness
            we're almost out of.

As for longevity, we'll leave that to oceans
            against which beating is not violence,
screaming not even noticeable.
And to the upright moonlight
        wherein ruins are most beautiful.
Then one sliding-glass dawn
            we will disappear
the way half-moons have before us
        that could not continue the carriage of light.
We'll loosen our last prints in the dust —
            not to be needlessly permanent.
But should this disappearance be taken
        for a fatal flaw in the plot?
                Or not?
Maybe it's just a further invention.

By the time you get here
Art will already be aimed at you,
       whole cities headed your way.
You'll arrive just in time
to see pages turned on their tethers
                or torn out,
and a language, perfectly fitted to your tongue,
         already in the use of others.

You, the unborn child —
a star that has burned for years without witness,
will arrive at last and burn no better here.

You will beat at the doors of home
and beg for a bondage you might happily assume.
You will cry to be carried
       or to be allowed to rest —
but it is better to run,
      and to rest while running, than to ride.
Beware of jockies
      with the strange undercarriage of birds,
and of hands bridled to a head's great weight.

Before long, most of your hosts will disappear.
A soft leather spotlight will play
       over the place where they stood.
In what brain will you be borne then?
In what synapse but your own will you move?
Although your mind may be fat as a pup
      you will always be hungry.
You will hunt in the parallel pines
       and find your direction
changed by memories it has
      already been changed by before.

Then lie down, if you like, among Neanderthals.
No need to wash excessively —
       an unclean death is unheard of,
          in any case.

You need have no fear of fake bears
    fed to you by wirephoto.
Nor of real teeth bared.
Nor of any news which,
    with baglike blows to the head,
       declares you worthless.
Remember what we've said:
The body is a pump for filling the mind
and a companion to its sorrow.
    You'll never be without it.

We celebrate
the insurrection of the celibates
                today, the first of May.
It's the date when
the old beholders of bifurcation
first ate the reddish fruit and said,
"It's from its own necessity
                that the apple grows,
and it's from *our* own
                that we eat it.
What's the matter with that?"

But where are the air-blue rugs now
that were to have borne us toward the homeland?
Where the sled dog with thick fur
and eyestripe that would have
                bearing on our lives?
The adder, still blind from
                his black hole, reels back
from our dazzling shins.
Our eyes will never line up again with his.

Hardboned hordes have
beat this land into legend,
the better to abandon it like a stone tsar.
And our function is to carry forth that fiction,
the better to turn away unconvinced.

So what's to celebrate?
                — Except that the great fruit still hangs
                    straight down from the tipped branch
                                like a tail at rest.
                — Except that the vegetables
                    exude the same old confidence
                                from their beds.

ALLELUIA CHORUS **2**

The light shifts its quarters in the smoke
exhaling charms of hoof and horn
         and disarming vaccines.
Thick as thistledust the moving plot cannot be caught
         nor swallowed
         nor thrown down, but
like a number, it keeps its unalterable weight.

I know how all of this will end:
More predictions will come to pass, and more,
but none to stay.
Until at last we're excused, these cowboys
and I, from each other.
To take leave of our senses
and search other mysteries less marred
         by impertinences.

Meanwhile, we concentrate on the face flickering there;
by face is meant, of course, that part turned this way.
The other side is not interesting
except to him who drowns there.
So in a cistern you've seen your own face
         recede with the season,
and behind the fallen features wondered
what black and diagonal beast is that
         passing through the wreckage?

But must we compose a whole creature
from a thin rider floating on the wall?
The source is dead and drifting,
and what need have we of a source anyway,
         who are already sated?
When even the black sky
         (of which there's surely only one)
                 is a redundance,
what can solace us for this abundance?
Or for these lighted plains
where we rock as if the earth's turning
              had stirred us.

I
In California,
ankle-high animals occupy the tablelands.
How many, going and coming from behind each other,
                              I cannot verify
(some ranging with insolence anywhere,
                         some never moving)
because my heart with its whips grows tired of pursuing
those creatures it cannot know it cannot know.

II
Men packed in slickers profess expertise
                    off the coasts of California.
Some say the sinking rain is a whole thing,
        torn when they get to it.
Some say it's a handful of random parts
        falling toward nomination.

III
Our heads are not pleased with these provisions;
bells ring, guns ring, rains strike simultaneities,
but we are not amused.
We say this place, where nothing is sacrilege, is no fun —
we want a better odds.
We want a sky clear again,
with a yellow hemisphere, of which
the rest can be guessed and the whole called MOON.

IV
In California,
the opposite of one hundred suns is none
                              (and of one, too).
No wonder we feel we have things in common here.
We cry out, "Count us, Father, we are the same.
Do not distinguish — how could you?
We're a funnel of numbers; at the bottom is zero,
at the top eight hundred thousand. Count us!"

V
Sometimes in California they say
              the earth is flat (meaning it's tasteless),
or they say it's round (meaning it's not flat),
and under the slender stone-game-of-rain it rolls
and relieves the air of instabilities.

VI
But our heads are not pleased with these divisions
                              in California.
Where our eyes drift aimlessly over the ground,
they're like wild ideas.
To what shall we apply them? To nothing for long,
for truly they are soothed with drifting.

To tell how my tent was torn,
       after seven years of sun and dust,
is to return to the day the threads gave way
       all in a perfect line.
Was ever a rip so perfect?
       A fault without flaw!
You who rejoice in symmetry will understand that.

And through the rip the rains came
       (collector of which I called river,
       collection of which I called sea),
and my strength was taxed
       while the weak waters ran free.

But, I said,
       our God holds to his own shape—
               triangular it is—
and we must imitate him.
And I lifted my pointed hands,
       and with a perfect patch
       destroyed the perfect tear.

Now I live in the hills among sheep
and my function is to ward off ills,
and to kill the oldtime wolves with slanted hides.
To kill all molesters of flocks, in fact,
       whose spines deviate from the perfect plumb.
What other acts can I commit in my meadow
                   but murder?

But to destroy the improper beasts—
       those with numberless teeth—
I must tear open the hide and let the life run out.
       (creator of which I called good,
       creation of which I could not).
And in the presence of a mind
       that holds to its own shape
       and makes no sound,
I must roll the body into a ditch downwind.
How strange what remains,

unsullied by systems other than solar,
and that only from afar.

But you who rejoice in symmetry will say:
It was perfect, was ever a death so perfect?
A fault without flaw.

Strangers came to our camp.
We knew them by their shadows
longer and cooler than the men.
And when they were gone,
we knew them by their having been here,
and by the even stranger absence before us.
It was the enemy, perhaps,
who has left a flat memory on our minds,
but, like the blind, we cannot find there
any rumor of the rounded master.

That's the mystery:
This whole background is a hole
into which others are sinking, but
we never seem to.
We pour fourteen deaths on the ground,
but nothing is found except
a cartridge belt cut from the waist of a captain,
or strings from the metal-ringed
eyes of his boots.

We suspect a passion's afoot here without person.
But we've searched the red-beasted wilderness
that shelters the mind from modernity,
and our attempts at contempt are laughed at.
Tonight our tents are tied down,
sails tied down, doors bolted against gales.
We don't need courage to survive this anymore.
It's surviving that encourages.

For two hours the leopard has lain
on his side, on his shelf,
his whole body no better than a foot,
                              asleep.
We have no interest in this,
                              we move on.
Such is the gift of the perfect beast,
that we may abandon him any time.

The rain is falling in spots,
everywhere in spots,
for the sakes of whom is it everlasting?
We are allowed to stand in line,
                    first outside,
                    then inside the PACHYDERMS.
Abandon the biographical plate —
disregard the date of birth and capture —
We, who are so absorbed in abundance,
                    have a whole bulk to consider,
and nothing stuns the brain
like this excess of evidence.

We look for old confrontations today.
Old, outright horrors,
the survival of which we are famous for.
To lift up the enormous head of escapee
and show mercy on the indigent,
                    that's what we want.
But each misfortune here counts only as one,
and the final one as one;
meanwhile, the tapping continues
                    and the raving on.

Coyotes cannot sit yet,
cannot cry out yet, who must wait
for a later time to salute the fat moon.
A time when what shapes the waves
                    will be eaten by them,

and the ruts will run on
         empty of their rays.

But the lion sits.
He turns like a beacon,
surprised by a thick crowd in the rocks.
         And still his light revolves,
unable to come to rest on this disaster.
Leaves us unlit long, for each flash discreet
that relieves itself of the sight of us sinking.

We listen to the intestinal sound in the ear.
Secrets are overdrawn there,
         a notice will be sent.
Meanwhile, keep the mind vacant—
Other animals will pass here soon.
         What falls into place behind them
will be altered, of course,
but it will seem similar.

They have not learned
         the whole truth, either,
about this place.
Do not even guess that a very large part
         is being saved for later consumption.
Such is the gift of the perfect beast.

Once all your thirteen hundred bones, stockstill,
sat like a thing not meant for dialogue
           (a demi-god in wait for a trout)
              a semi-infinity.
Your shadow seemed strange by its hollowness,
                by its shifting edges
that carried you from stillness to stillness.
And by the way your hands collected over it
their two twilights.

Once like Adam you pointed to God.
And like God he pointed back,
and arrowheads entered and left your profile
                 without a trace
except an occasional feather. Until, at last,
              accidentally,
something was trapped behind the pane
            facing out,
so wild to break its crystal rider.

How many times did you think "bird," before
it was noticed it was you who thought it?
And how many times "I," before that, too,
              flew into the air?
But the way the mortal birds move through,
the air might not be there.

Out over northern hills
the wild grass takes leave of its green,
flung back by some night moving hoof.
Oh don't you know how to portion the herd,
the austere white oxen of your stare?

These nights whizz by with the intensity
             of falling objects.
And you're dazed by their absence of dialect,
by their aimless altitudes beating against you
like original blood,
        abroad,
           in need of a body to bear it.

Proud of my pride,
I grew fat and romantic,
I grew rich in revenge and loved animals.
A nature walk was a kind of
            Belgian bestiary brought with me
where one tapestried foot at a time
            was woven to the ground,
where my hounds followed face down
like surface swimmers unable to drown,
            and I knew I'd brought
it all with me —
all already there in the restless bodies of my eyes
rolling in their oval recesses.

I liked my nature green and
didn't care how it got that way.
It's a mistake to always ask,
            Is it alive, is it dead? Where's the heart?

I crushed the feeding grass
feeding, feeding — what egotism! — until it fails
            in a whole field of feeding.
How can I know when it dies anyway?
Except that nothing's refreshed
            that doesn't die a little.

It was a place like this, I suppose,
where the original nudes, wrong in their
            kindness to each other,
suffered their great loss at the hands of an adder,
and the four darknesses converged on them
and the black tenderness
            began digesting them horribly.

But this is all a tale told by a head to a head
of how the weeds came up like animals out of the dirt
and grew larger —
            their chief act, in fact —
            and how they found me
like a prey to an older prey
whose reverence for reverence grows bigger each day
and less fastidious.

"One joy is not enough.
          We must have several."
Their majesties came ashore in hammocks
among birds and traveling boxes.
We carried cabin chairs to the sand.
But the lords were disconsolate, and
their ladies emitted common nouns.

That visit, Easter breads were eaten
          with the head thrown back.
And porter was poured from beneath
                              its foam —
          three glasses it took to make
                              one clear.
In the dark the ship creaked and commanded us
                              to hear.
Or it was still and we commanded ourselves?

The bells rang with eleven interruptions.
And their majesties read the spaces,
and they read the sounds,
and they disdained to sleep so soon.

They oversaw the reconstruction of a new moon
after an earlier model of a moon.
And when it was done they dedicated it
                              to themselves.
But in a fortnight it was gone again,
and their majesties gone on, too,
                              to new spheres.

Now the standard birds stand in the branches,
each peculiar to its own place.
They've changed, probably, but not noticeably —
there being no joy in that information
nor joy in recounting it.

From the very first
we could hardly keep up with the insights
gained by the light of your power saws.
Eyes making slots in the air;
teeth dispatching secrets.
You were fast as an Aztec to the heart of things here,
but still you complained.
You complained that the veins that stood out
           on the sides of the sacrifice
               were drained, and that your
blade was turning white.
You complained that the wind was cold at night,
and that the sourdough rose too slowly
like a soul out of its loaf pan.

You thought this land was like the fatty heart of a lamb,
red and white and wholly edible,
but what of the facewounds,
the fleshwounds that are part of your profession?
What of the price you must pay
in order that the phenomena may
           fall back like slaves before you?

Today, when you dazzle us
with the caps-of-chrome that cover your hubs
           and make them more beautiful,
we try to remember
that once you were the divine Goths who meddled
among the trees.
We will admit you were splendid
           in your thousand leaves, but
now that the land is clear,
tell us, what are we meant to do here?
How shall we fill up the spaces between us?
And how address the simple air that is left
           whose surface is too porous
                 to rest against
and whose center is unimportant?

When I saw how, without wind,
the moon was moved to grow more perfect
                              I became ambitious.
I sold myself for miniature monies,
        (those with the heads of men and tails of eagles).
Later I had a chance to buy myself back
                              with those abominations,
but, like a virgin, I shook my head,
                              screaming manifestoes.
I would not give up my coins,
        (those with the men stamped sideways,
                              and sometimes
a full-figured woman carrying an armful of grain).

When I saw how, without wind,
the moon was moved to diminish
                              I wondered what had been lost.
Or had it only escaped *me*, for whom it was no
                              fit companion?
I slept, as usual,
        on the sides of my forehead,
and my dreams, as usual,
        were like brown rings worn in the grass
                              by a clockwise dancer.
During the day, I pursued my monies and their men,
        (those who stare out of their circles
                              toward the time
they were made, not this way, but at something
                              that happened then).
I, too, would turn my profile
        but for whom save the full face?

Recently I've noticed how, without moon,
the sky has grown perfect.
It no longer escapes me
        that it was to vanish my innocence came here;
my hands grow passionate on the sides of food,
I try to bring to myself what I want,

try not to bring too much.
Now what I wonder is, what part of my loot
                              will outlive me
                      and what part be lost?
I foresee that the nose and the cheek
                       will be rubbed away first
by the erosion of many whereabouts,
and that nothing's recognized when only the eyes
                                  are left
        staring out of a blob of silver.

What a mania for megalith-moving
or rather for megalith-making
                            by moving big rocks
out of the way of sunrise!
But it's the shadow-shift that stirs us the most
and the unexpected rectitudes of men
bent enough to be born, but
not bogged by colossal modesties.

Bonfires played a big part
in luring us to them.
Like slow moving edibles
                            we enter the pen of shades,
where sunlit smoke is more solid than pillars,
where water that falls
                            acquits its place
leaving legends for later
of extinct moving parts.

We came down from London for sunrise,
laughed-at-lame-children of a long language,
to look back through magnificent gaps,
to play ancients-grown-transparent
                            plunged in their prophesies.

Like them we languish on paths
                    hardened by handed-down hooves.
Reappraise the rock-breaking,
                    rock-hauling,
                    upended centuries.
Or, lying among lizards, we loaf
in our slowed-down engines of skin.
Knowing we can't be tipped
                    equipped as we are,
an outriggered race
better braced than boulders
                    for marking this plain.

The cow walks away from him,
        gives up her immensity,
        letting it die before his very eyes—
and acquires a new smallness
        that fits her nature perfectly.
And in Aquinas what dies also
        are those details of udder and eyelid,
        changed while he watches
            into legs and head.

            But he cannot leave it yet.
To be forced to forsake the end
without foreseeing the beginning,
        it's impossible!
And this middle which he wishes to keep
        and yet is not yet complete,
will be added to every minute
        until it, too, is destroyed.

For he shall not be able to imagine it
        when he leaves here:
The rain that falls on the rock
        (which hurts the foot)
            seems harder than
the rain that falls on the grass.
Recognition of rock and of cow, too,
        are mixed together,
but to predict what shall move away
        and what shall stay fixed,
he must separate them again:
        the cow to move out mixed with rain
            and the rock to remain.

And the face of this field is acre needed
to furnish a place over which its time may pass
and against which its ticking may be heard.
It's the fixity that speaks!
Rocks resting like Roman numerals, without which

hands could move in space forever,
                unreadable.
Thomas, seeing himself in the little pond as wavy,
guesses his original is straight but not seen
                standing nearby.
In the water or on it,
        he sees the water, too,
and separates out the wonder from the wet
                and names its cause.

It's a very old goods
        that has the fable sewn sideways,
with sky thicker than fleshtone
        and heavy as rider.
A hat drifts toward us, headless —
        what's most wanted wanting:
a face slipped out sidesaddle
        too subtle to show the bluish blood.

His place is kept though,
        surrounded but not soaked up
by red handkerchief,
by guitar made of different thread.

He would age if he could
        but there's nothing he can turn into.
Must fit back into himself somehow,
back into the fine rigged shape
        made like a ship
           through the neck of a bottle.

Yarn of a single sewer
        grows muscular beneath him.
Her gift was to lift the horizon,
        lying loose in its furrow,
and let him ride through the vegetable dyes.
And to leave him:
        her lover, brought to our eyes
        on beakfuls of pale thread.

ALLELUIA CHORUS **3**

In these,
it was to catch the cannon-colored elephants
              outside Johannesburg.
To freeze the grassfires that feed on the mind
              until it is gone.
Later, with magnifying glass,
      it is to examine the ash of former acts.
It was no accident:
          that oxygen beyond understanding,
              that light that never dried.
The sky was savage in its demands:
One cloud held up,
one cloud cut off and dripping.
And still, like self-stirred mammals,
              the months passed.
And, without coaching, the memory grew saintlier.
Let it hang from its heels like a hide —
          Let it be photographed!

In these,
the brown boy by the wagon cannot run
              but there is no need.
The shadow that holds him in place
goes under the master's hand and into the woods
              where reversible roles are begun.
Appetites, stockpiled against the horizon,
may tow him out of his childhood,
Or he may be diminished by now at the anklebones,
      but he will never slip *these* irons.

It is no accident
          that eyes sleep the sleep of vandals,
              ignorant of their loot.
Tomorrow, these albums filled with trees,
          filled with fruit and the juices of fruit,
              will be broken into —
Filled with bees that give off dangerous rays,

and a whole live-load of days let down
on sensitive paper.

Let them praise these ashes,
who come too late to feel the fire.
And praise the spirits cut loose like balloons,
each its own propellant for soaring,
for seeing this place as small.
Before their own faces sink
like moonlight through the drinking water,
they will sleep the sleep of vandals, too.
And awake with corrected vision.
Sound, but more savage than before.

I
You don't ask one who is dying
                        the name of his hour
                        or how he recommends it.
You don't ask him to breathe deeply
                        first in and then out —
he knows what he's doing.
He knows that the tides
                        are forced to follow forever
                        the moon's repetitious route.
And that he is not.

He will tell you how, at noon,
the waves arrived like crazed teams.
                        How, by five-fifteen,
they'd won what they wanted and withdrew.
                        For the record,
that's when his attention began to drag
                        like a stylus against the
unbreakable silence.

II
At five-thirty he began to complain:
How, at birth, the bridges were blown up behind him.
How the streets were blinded at their ends.
How the animals would not eat what he offered,
would not let him pet them.
                        (They knew better than he did
                        what they wanted him to be.)
Like a god, he complained that it was a *found world*
which he did not savor.
Would rather have labored for it.
Rather have saved up and planned for it.
And done without the *luck.*

III
What time is it now?
Spring must be a long way off —
But he would want us to plant, at once,

the four-week-old body of a Dutch bulb,
           smelling of dynamite.
He would want us to care for his car
           that coughs like a foundling
               he dared not destroy.
And for his silk purse, that pricked up
        at the sounds of our squealing.
He would want us to drag his gold, unconscious,
        from its bed.

IV
But we're getting ahead of him a little,
with our hopsack knapsacks,
with our diamonds shifting on false bottoms.
A hundred of us, ahead of him each day,
and none erased to furnish a place
           for the next hundred to rest.
No wonder his shadow is showing less profit.
No wonder his spirit is sprawling like water,
having learned nothing
           from its years of containment.
He's trying to rise, but
you don't ask one who is dying
           to restrain himself.
He knows what he's doing.
He's seen, from birth, how the earth
           mills about in its skies,
grinding down what grows thereon.
And he's guessed all along
that it's in order not to become too big,
                perhaps.

For four days he drifted
>in a human boat, knotted at both ends
>>to keep out the light.
And the sun was wasted.
And the rain was wasted.
Even death was wasted on Lazarus
>that might have been instructive
>>somewhere else.
During that time
>what furrowed the inward air was not eye,
more like arrow toward narrowed lids
>and beyond.
He marked the walls
>as the hopping chalk commanded.
He tapped on pipes but got no reply,
>except the sounds of powders falling.
When halftimbered faces of mourners
>>collapsed around him
he could not help them, because
the barely perceptible soul upwind of his body
>>could not support sunlight,
and because his old estate
>was melting away like snow
that would not pack, would not hold his weight.

Then for some reason
the whole costly colony started up again —
became the heart's ideal again —
>arrived at by rooted runner.
And his brain, piled like a rope in the dark,
>>apart from understanding,
was tugged forward.
Winebottle winds poured over his wounds,
and all textures without memory

made way for his savage denseness.
BLESS THE ANTHRACITE FROM WHICH RED IS TAKEN
BLESS THE ROPES HOPPING ON THEIR ENDS
AND THE BELLS THAT LIFT THEM.

Out of the ground, with his coat carried before him
like a folded map—
Out of the long superfluity of sleep
unwinding white as Arabia,
to mark the sun again as the stone alone
left unturned.
Now, like all for whom breath is necessary to begin,
and the end of it to end,
he fishes the wind for word of his fame.
To catch in his own name
the restitution he can
for that lost silence.

I
We remove your canvas cover,
is this not better than before?
You are given a license to
            draw on exposed rocks,
and so that workmanlike waves
            should not be wasted
you are given a pencil.

You are the hand-carried hawk
            whose hunt we have come to watch.
To see sorrows wolfed down,
            only half ripe,
that cause howling in the night.
To see the cavity where a mind is kept
approached by fingerless forces.

We would follow your Israelite flight
wherever the evidence divides,
(all the seas on the sides,
            all the oaks under O)
but after you pass
            there's a crashing behind you
of waters re-rooting at random
and of mouths closing on leaves.

In this shifting place
even the rigidity of nouns
            must respond to ponderous wrenches.
If we build a little castle
            out of patted sand,
how long can it stand, before
            failing in loyalty to itself?

We have brought you here
            because our arks are not adequate —
not against waves of anti-architect.
What we want are your eyes,

                better built than boats
         to carry us over the things we see
                        without sinking.

You are the lion,
         lighted from the inside,
whose pride we are.
We roar, lifting a squat wind your way.
We disorder the air before our mouths
so that fur is no longer tranquil.

II
To have a face —
To have a face painted on the lid of a box —
What more is necessary for immortality?
So what if your head is worn down
                    to bare shoulders.
So what if darkness reaches out of your eyes
                        like oars,
pulling you past the lighted objects.

Something is being born.
Like clothes that have lain
         painfully in a crowded trunk
it is lifted and shaken out.
A memory begins —
A red microscope memory
         of camps ripped up
                and numbly flapping.
Of an old three-holed heart
so durable we've dared forget it.

We don't care if the things you bring
         have their numbers filed off —
some perhaps stolen.
We will perform ceremonies over them anyway
like those before the doors of surgery:
Our gloves, red but steady,
         opening the slotted texts.

New worlds will fall forward
        like acts without engines,
and we will wear them smooth
        with our leaning, with
our sailing back and forth.

We hope you are refreshed with your hood removed—
We hope you are pleased
        with our oval hands held up
                like howling-shells
and benedictions launched between.
There's a twelve-mile-long opportunity
             for mercy here,
we hope you will not waste it.

To each wild mutation we say,
THROW BACK YOUR HEAD, IF YOU HAVE ONE, AND HOWL
       WE ARE WILLING TO LISTEN.
We are all amateurs here —
       horrors hatched by earthquake.
If ridicule rides the grooves of our arms
       out to the ends and beyond,
don't be offended. We approve. Approve!
But manual laughter is too tiring
       and besides,
what are applause machines for
       if not to assist us in our loving?

 A knife arrives with note attached:
SELL YOUR VICES, GET NEW ONES, THESE ARE NOT SOUND.
Further instructions for the use of the knife
       are not announced.
Are *we* not the owners then?
We, who to keep the earth clean of hours
       must ourselves devour them.
(Are we not the fuel for catching fire
       while everything else goes free?)
With what else then,
stumped by a harvest neither large nor golden,
       can we come by amusing foods?

There may be a king folded neatly in the chest
but it gives no advantage.
Not when a reincarnation scare is on.
Why does everything rush to get on the right lists?
Why all the eager repeaters?
Something must have happened to hierarchy here
when even the victims show no resentment
       at not being men.

In virgin forests we forbid ourselves
       to light a fire.
For to drag the spirits, however undamaged,
       from their log,

is to manipulate the methane mysteries,
             and forever smell of brimstone.
Are we goats then, to be gotten?
             Or grandmothers
knitting up new hides for the young?
If even the bodies we bury underground
             cannot overcome their own wildness —
If even the fires finish nothing,
how will this place ever be done?

In spite of all the gushings
of grasses and waves, etc.,
it's hard to say what's being expressed.
A madness for further momentum, maybe.
And, without any special loathing
            for the knowness-of-here
a certain bicycle-envy is brought
to bikes ridden,
to bikes walked by faithful masters.

Bushes are blurred because
heads are bent forward like open-end shells
speeding toward a meeting of small periscopes.
What's expected of that rendezvous
I don't remember.
(The art of conversation?
Brilliant western words flaring up?
Lenses sweeping, giving off warmth?)

There's still time in the eye's honored ignorance
for shirts to blow without thinking
            into the sea.
Or for the small dark of a far shark
to impress the quilted waters.
But since everyone has come to count on
the plumped-up air to carry him forward
riders rarely go there anymore.

Actually, I never thought they'd get this far,
treading pedals as if they were water.
Or that, on pure ingenuity, their lives would be made up
out of whatever was on hand.
No wonder the inadvertant observance of this
is cause for unrest.

How much older can they get without strategy,
the space they take up wearing out,
            falling in folds about their wheels?
Feverish stars pass faster than ever

making intelligence seem silly —
       less than waves, less than grass.
Already half the future has arrived
and the rest is a mob on the horizon.
When these masters of solitude enter the winds
       and kick away the chocks,
what help is a head in all this,
       bent forward?
Less than a left arm lifted, probably,
or legs adrift already, moving by themselves.

I

If, as it says in the log,
there was just one big ark for all,
tall enough for giraffes,
long and clear enough for salmon,
then how fortunate the roundness
                    of its foundation —
that no edge was ever come to
                    much less fallen off.

Certain inadmissible certainties
                    were not admitted though,
which led to later enquiries . . . .
Instead, hives were brought aboard
to afford sweetness and the clarities made by instinct.
Sometimes interest in syllables diminished
                    to just two a word
which was enough
providing the treatment of subjects was not lavish.
It was then, when everything was mixed together,
that they had to be careful to remain
in the delicate halves of themselves —
                    the brain was not perfected.

II

But there's a chance —
                    just a chance —
that among the unsupervised who remained ashore
                    some survived!
Living in national forests
or clinging to mountaintops
                    like self-taught sheep.
If so, all that was unconsumed was theirs;
                    the cold, the toothmarked, the dark.
And when winds died down
they would have been the first to hear
                    the slippage of light earthward.
And to say, 'This place is hourly more ours than ever.'
Or, entering the molten future
                    at whatever edge first grew firm enough,

'The days of clay await our commands.'
There are delvers who will tell you
they could have taken comfort in roots
and other small sweet originals
                on which their hands had been trained.

And if the two groups were held apart by binoculars,
the glass, tough as woven water,
                would not have allowed them to drink.
Not at the places the old certainties were found.
The assumption is that sumptuous mists
                hid them from view;
the idlers from the ivory-voiced voyagers.
The log is not clear about this.

III
If, as it seems, all pasts
                once fattened-on are flattened
like killed leathers,
then it is only the portable names
                that are carried forward.
Names of the fathers
and of the high-looking, handsome brothers,
                carved on a stone or a log.
But the great veiled gauges are kept out of sight
by which their perfections were measured.

One thing is certain
the coasts are crowded with survivors of something!
Who, missing an earlier, arrowy death
now lie in a strange century
wondering at a pain in the chest.
Survivors who cannot remember arriving
                nor re-arriving.
Cannot remember any actions, actually,
only the position of the actors
                on a motionless sea.

IV
Like doors that wander away from their frames
the old days never fit back again.
In their place is a different distance

DATE DUE